A Word From the Author... (okay, a few words)...

Hi!

Here's your own handy pocket guide about the great state of West Virginia! It really will fit in a pocket–I tested it. And it really will be useful when you want to know a fact you forgot, to bone up for a test, or when your teacher says, "I wonder . . ." and you have the answer–instantly! Wow, I'm impressed!

Get smart, have fun!

Carole Marsh

West Virginia Basics explores your state's symbols and their special meanings!

West Virginia Geography digs up the what's where in your state!

West Virginia History is like traveling through time to some of your state's great moments!

West Virginia People introduces you to famous personalities and your next-door neighbors!

West Virginia Places shows you where you might enjoy your next family vacation!

West Virginia Nature - no preservatives here, just what Mother Nature gave to West Virginia!

All the real fun stuff that we just HAD to save for its own section!

Who Named You?

West Virginia's official state name is...

West Virginia

OFFICIAL: appointed, authorized, or approved by a government or organization

Statehood: June 20, 1863

West Virginia was the 35th state to join the Union.

A Name of Royal Proportions!

West Virginia got its name when the western counties of Virginia separated from the state during the Civil War because their people did not want to secede from the Union. Virginia was named by Sir Walter Raleigh for Queen Elizabeth I, the Virgin Queen. Several other names were considered for West Virginia, including Kanawha, Allegheny, and Augusta, but the citizens stuck with West Virginia because they were proud of the Virginian heritage.

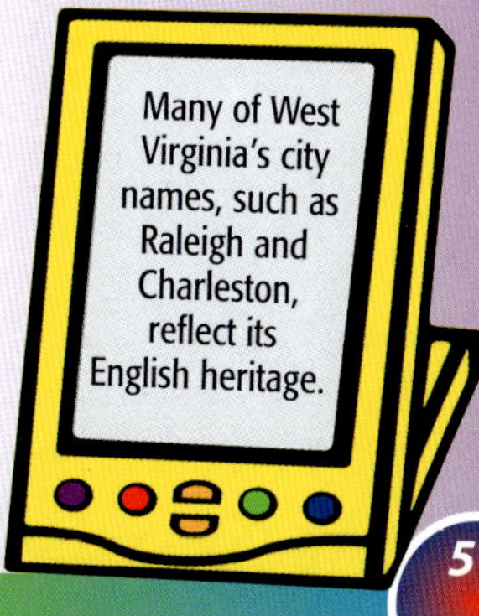

WHO Are You Calling Names?

West Virginia is not the only name by which our state is recognized. Like many other states, West Virginia has some nicknames, official or unofficial!

Mountain State

Panhandle State

State Capital: Charleston

Established 1788

First became capital of West Virginia in 1870

When West Virginia first broke off from Virginia and became a state in the Union in 1863, Wheeling was named the capital.

Charleston started out in 1788 as a frontier post called Fort Lee. It was settled by Scots-Irish and German immigrants. The community was named Charles Town in honor of the father of Colonel George Clendenin, who built Fort Lee. By 1818, this got shortened to Charleston. Charleston incorporated in 1870 and served as West Virginia's capital from 1870 until 1875 and became the permanent capital in 1885. Today, Charleston is West Virginia's largest city.

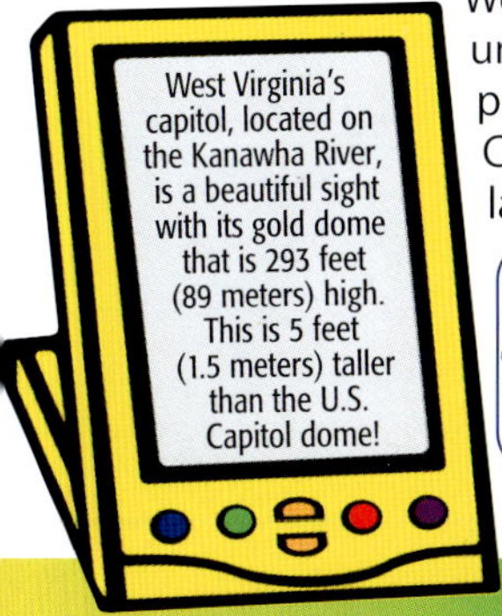

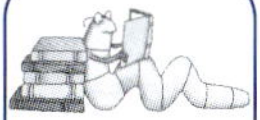

Word Definition

CAPITAL: a town or city that is the official seat of government

CAPITOL: the building in which the government officials meet

Who's in Charge Here?

West Virginia's GOVERNMENT has three branches:

- **EXECUTIVE**: A governor, secretary of state, state auditor, state treasurer, attorney general, commissioner of agriculture, state department heads
- **LEGISLATIVE**: Two Houses: The Senate (34 members); House of Delegates (100 members)
- **JUDICIAL**: Supreme Court (5 members), Circuit courts, Magistrate courts

The number of legislators is determined by population, which is counted every 10 years; thenumbers above are certain to change as West Virginia grows and prospers!

State Flag

West Virginia's current state flag was adopted in 1929. It features the state seal on a white background with a blue border. A red banner at the top of the seal says, "State of West Virginia." A wreath of the West Virginia state flower, rhododendron, surrounds the bottom of the seal.

As you travel throughout West Virginia, count the times you see the West Virginia flag! Look for it on government vehicles, too!

State Seal & Motto

State Seal

The state seal of West Virginia features a farmer and a miner standing next to a boulder with June 20, 1863, inscribed in it. This is the date West Virginia became a state. The boulder symbolizes the state's strength, steadfastness, and stability. Two rifles in front of the rock, topped by a Liberty Cap, serve as a reminder of West Virginians' willingness to fight for freedom. "State of West Virginia" and the state motto encircle the outside of the sea.

Word Definition MOTTO: a sentence, phrase, or word expressing the spirit or purpose of an organization or group

State Motto

West Virginia's state motto is...

Montani Semper Liberi

It means "Mountaineers are Always Free" in Latin.

Birds of a Feather

The state bird of West Virginia is the cardinal. It's known for its bright plumage and cheerful song. The male cardinal has bright red feathers, and the female is brown with a red beak.

The cardinal is the only Eastern red bird with a crest!

State Tree

State Tree

Sugar maples are an important part of West Virginia life. Every year, West Virginians produce maple syrup from the sugar maple trees, in a process called "sug'rin." The sap is collected from the trees and then boiled in a sugarhouse to make the syrup. The sugar maple is also valuable in its use for making furniture.

Big Laurel

A lovelier flower on earth was never sown.
—William Wordsworth

The *Rhododendron maximum,* or big laurel, was named the state flower of West Virginia in 1903 after public schools students encouraged legislators to do so. This flower belongs to the heath family and has large, dark evergreen leaves and pale pink or white blooms that are flecked with red or yellow.

RIDDLE:

If the state flower got mixed up with the state bird, what would you have?

ANSWER: A cardinal that's got evergreen leaves–it could happen!

State Animal

BLACK BEAR

The black bear isn't really black at all but rather a deep brown color. West Virginia black bears mainly live in the eastern mountain region, but black bears are common in 36 other states and Canada. Black bears can grow 5 to 6 feet (1.5 to 1.8 meters) tall.

Black bears have an excellent sense of smell, which makes up for their poor vision and hearing.

Chalcedony

West Virginia's state gem, chalcedony (pronounced kal–séd–nee), is not really a gem, but rather a fossil coral. It can be found in Hillsdale limestone deposits in West Virginia's Pocahontas and Greenbrier counties.

Chalcedony is a fine-grained form of quartz. It occurs in a variety of colors, including blue-white, buff, light tan, gray, yellow, or brown. Iron oxides will cause chalcedony to be colored red or green. There are many varieties of chalcedony, including agate, onyx, bloodstone, and carnelian.

Chalcedony is said to have special properties that make its wearer feel kind, friendly, strong, and emotionally balanced. It's also said to ward off hostility, irritability, and bad feelings!

Chalcedony was used as a sacred stone in Native American ceremonies.

MONONGAHELA SILT LOAM

In 1997, West Virginia designated Monongahela silt loam as its state soil. This soil is mainly yellowish brown or grayish brown. Because it drains well, it is good soil for pasture lands, crops, and industrial and residential uses.

OLD GOLD AND BLUE

West Virginia's state colors are old gold and blue. These were named by West Virginia legislators in 1963. Can you decide a reason why West Virginians chose these for their state colors?

Golden Delicious Apple

West Virginia legislators named the apple as the West Virginia state fruit in 1972, but in 1995, they amended this to specify the Golden Delicious apple as the state fruit. West Virginia apple farmers were the first to grow this particular variety.

Golden Delicious apples are large yellow apples that are crisp, sweet, and juicy. They're a good apple to use in cooking and also good for apple juice and applesauce.

State Songs

West Virginia has three state songs, but the official one is "The West Virginia Hills," with words and music by H.E. Engle and Ellen King.

Oh, the West Virginia hills!
How majestic and how grand,
With their summits bathed in glory,
Like our Prince Immanuel's land!
Is it any wonder then,
That my heart with rapture thrills,
As I stand once more with loved ones
On those West Virginia hills?
Oh the hills,
Beautiful hills.
How I love the West Virginia hills!
If o'er sea or land I roam
Still I'll think of happy home,
And the friends among the West Virginia hills.

West Virginia's other two state songs are "West Virginia, My Home Sweet Home," by Julian G. Hearne, Jr., and "This Is My West Virginia," by Iris Bell.

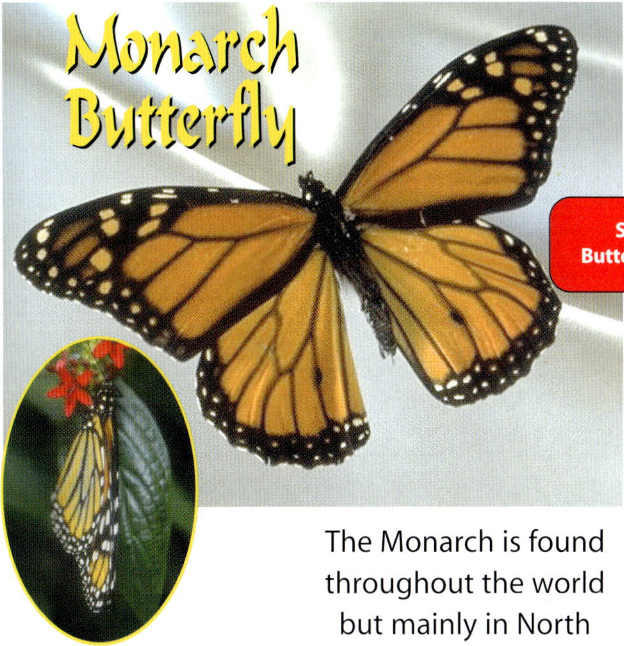

State Butterfly

The Monarch is found throughout the world but mainly in North America. Each fall, monarch butterflies migrate south to California, Florida, and Mexico. In its two-year life span, the monarch makes the trip twice.

Butterflies cannot fly if their body temperature is less than 86°F (30°C). At air temperatures below this, they must "warm up" their flight muscles by sunning their bodies or shivering their wings.

Brook Trout

State Fish

Brook trout are native to West Virginia waters and this fish is one anglers love to catch! It's quite a fighter for its size. Brook trout do well in West Virginia's clear, cold spring-fed streams, but not in warmer waters. This trout variety has olive-colored sides and can easily be identified because of its light-colored lower fin edges. Male brook trout have a reddish belly.

West Virginia Brook Trout

Kids, get an adult to help you prepare this recipe.

Put a trout filet on foil. Drizzle with lemon juice. Sprinkle with salt and pepper. Add shredded smoked ham and broil fish until done.

The State of West Virginia

Mountain ridges and rivers form West Virginia's borders. This may be the most irregularly shaped state in the nation!

State Location

West Virginia is one of the Appalachian states.

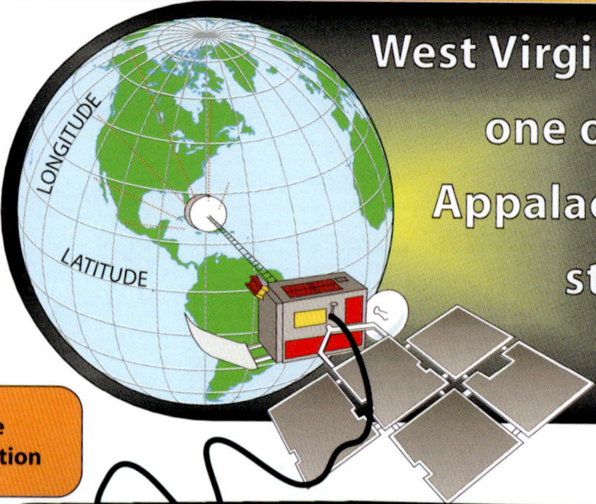

State Location

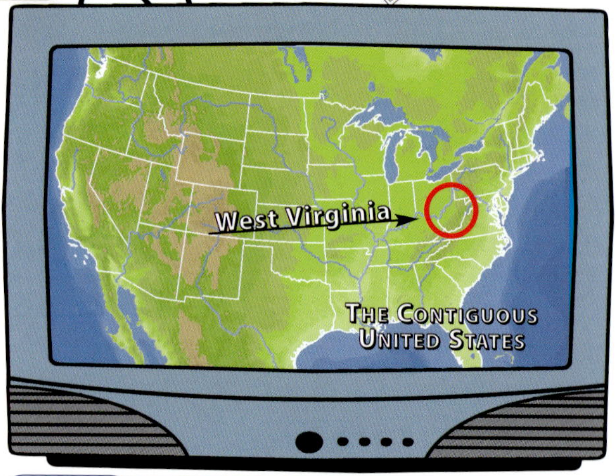

Word Definition

LATITUDE: Imaginary lines which run horizontally east and west around the globe
LONGITUDE: Imaginary lines which run vertically north and south around the globe

On The Border!

These border West Virginia:

States:	Ohio Maryland Kentucky	Pennsylvania Virginia

River: Ohio River

I'll Take the Low Road...

West Virginia stretches 237 miles (381 kilometers) from north to south—or south to north. Either way, it's a long drive!

Total Area: Approximately 24,231 square miles (62,753 square kilometers)

Land Area: Approximately 24,087 square miles (62,381 square kilometers)

West Virginia is 265 miles (426 kilometers) from east to west—or west to east. Either way, it's *still* a long drive!

You Take the High Road!

Highest Point

Spruce Knob—4,861 feet (1,482 meters)

Spruce Knob gets its name from the red spruce trees on Spruce Mountain. This tree produces a gum that was the ancestor to today's chewing gum!

Lowest Point

The Potomac River in Harpers Ferry—240 feet (73 meters)

I'm County-ing on You!

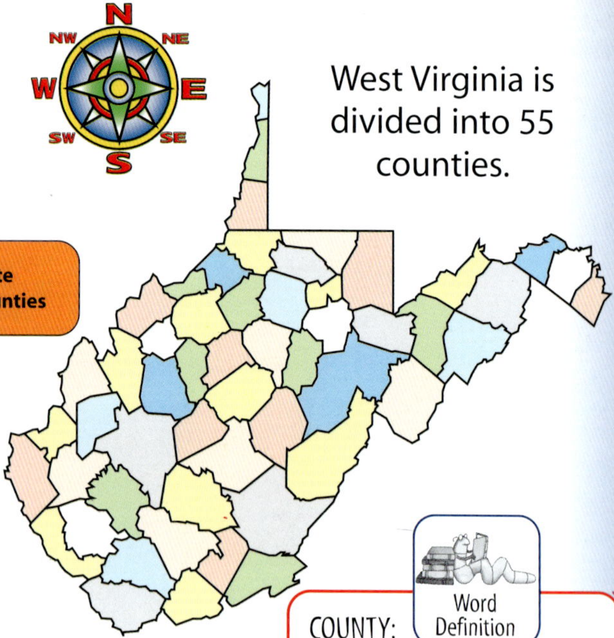

West Virginia is divided into 55 counties.

Word Definition

COUNTY: an administrative subdivision of a state or territory

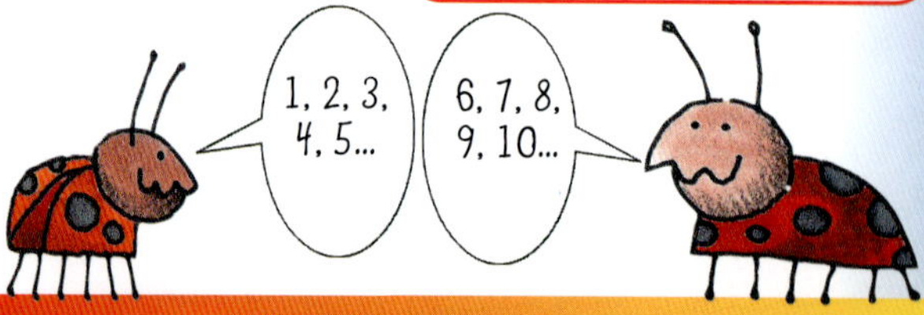

Natural Resources

It's All Natural!

Forests make up about 12,128,000 acres (4,908,202 hectares) in West Virginia. More than 80 percent of the state is covered by timber.

Word Definition

NATURAL RESOURCES: things that exist in or are formed by nature

Rocks and Minerals:

Bituminous (soft) coal
Natural gas
Brine
Rock salt
Limestone
Sand
Clay
Sandstone
Shale
Iron ore

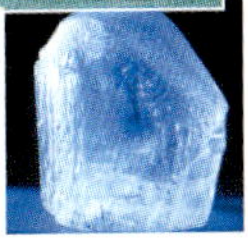

Weather, Or Not?!

West Virginia's temperatures average 22°F (-5.5°C) in the mountains in winter and 83°F (28.3°C) in the summer.

Highest temperature: 112°F (44.4°C), Martinsburg, July 10, 1936

°F=Degrees Fahrenheit °C=Degrees Celsius

Lowest temperature: -37°F (-38.3°C), Lewisburg, December 30, 1917

Bluefield, West Virginia, calls itself "nature's air-conditioned city." Merchants serve free lemonade if the temperature reaches 90°F (32°C)—but that doesn't happen very often.

Topography

Back on Top

West Virginians claim their state is so mountainous that if you ironed out their state, it would cover the entire country! West Virginia's topography includes:

Appalachian Plateau

Allegheny Front

Ridge and Valley Region

Blue Ridge

Word Definition

TOPOGRAPHY: the detailed mapping of the features of a small area or district

West Virginia is the only state that lies completely within the Appalachian Mountains.

King of the Hill

Allegheny Mountains
Shenandoah Mountains
Appalachian Mountains
Bald Knob
Bickett Knob
Buckhorn Knob
Cheat Mountain
Cow Knob
Cook Mountain
Guyandot Mountain
Laurel Mountain
Mount Desert
Peters Mountain
Piney Swamp Knob
Rich Mountain

Down The River

Here are some of West Virginia's major rivers:

- Ohio River
- Big Sandy River
- Little Kanawha River
- New River
- Gauley River
- Elk River
- Coal River
- Monongahela River
- Potomac River
- Greenbrier River

Gone Fishin'

Major Lakes

- Summersville Lake
- Sutton Lake
- Bluestone Lake
- Tygart Lake
- East Lynn Lake

West Virginia has no natural lakes. Locks and dams have been used to create these reservoirs.

RESERVOIR: a body of water stored for public use

Word Definition

ARE YOU A CITY MOUSE... OR A COUNTRY MOUSE?

Have you heard of these wonderful West Virginia town, city, or crossroad names? Perhaps you can start your own list!

MAJOR CITIES:

- Charleston
- Huntington
- Wheeling
- Parkersburg
- Morgantown
- Weirton
- Fairmont
- Clarksburg
- Beckley
- Bluefield

UNIQUE NAMES:

- Boomer
- Confidence
- Cyclone
- Duo
- Exchange
- Harmony
- Hurricane
- Paw Paw
- Quick
- Red Jacket
- Tornado
- Uneeda
- Windy

Transportation

Major Interstate Highways

I-79
I-77
I-64
I-70
I-68
I-81

Major Airport

Yeager Airport, Charleston

Transpor-
tation

Railroads

West Virginia has about 4,000 miles (6,436 kilometers) of railroad track today. Railroads are mostly used to export coal out of the state.

Chief Riverport

Huntington

Other

Personal Rapid Transit, West Virginia University, Morgantown—electrically powered system that moves WVU students around campus

Timeline

1606	King James grants charter that includes what is now West Virginia
1669	John Lederer and comrades first see West Virginia
1671	Thomas Batts, Robert Fallam explore Blue Ridge, Allegheny Mountains to New River
1731	Morgan ap Morgan becomes area's first white settler with cabin at Bunker Hill
1742	John Peter Salling finds coal on the Coal River
1747	George Washington surveys western Virginia lands
1773	First permanent settlement started in Kanawha Valley
1859	John Brown and followers raid federal arsenal at Harpers Ferry; Brown is captured, convicted of treason, and hanged
1861	Counties in western Virginia won't secede with Virginia; propose separate state of West Virginia
1863	West Virginia becomes the nation's 35th state
1866	West Virginia won't reunite with Virginia at end of Civil War
1885	Capital is moved to Charleston, where it remains today
1891	Hatfields, McCoys end their bitter feud
1915	U.S. Supreme Court rules West Virginia owes Virginia debt from when it separated in 1863
1959	National Radio Astronomy Observatory begins operations at Green Bank
1965	West Virginia legislature passes environmental laws
2001	West Virginia enters the 21st century!

Here come the humans!

Thousands of years ago, ancient peoples inhabited West Virginia. They may have originally come across a frozen bridge of land between Asia and Alaska. If so, they slowly traveled east until some settled in what would one day become the state of West Virginia.

The Kanawha River Valley in West Virginia first became home to Indians about 12,500 years ago. As the climate became warmer, the tribes moved from hunting and gathering food to learning to grow some crops. They became less likely to move and started their own villages.

Native Americans Once Ruled!

Archaeologists are certain that Indian tribes were living in the West Virginia area as long ago as 12,000 years. They have found stone tools, sharp spear points, and pieces of pottery that date back to that period. Another piece of evidence of West Virginia's earliest inhabitants are its earthen mounds.

Several thousand years ago, groups of Indians known as the Adena and Hopewell began constructing large mounds of earth in which they buried their dead leaders. First, the dead would be placed in log tombs and then covered in dirt. Some larger mounds have several layers of tombs and dirt. For some unexplained reason, the mound builders left their villages around AD 1500. Experts think disease, drought, or other tribes could have chased them away.

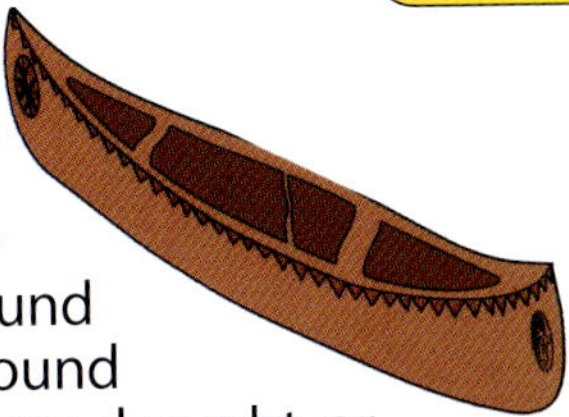

When European explorers arrived in the early 1700s, they found Tuscarora, Mingo, Shawnee, and Delaware. These tribes all belonged to the mighty Iroquois Confederacy.

Word Definition

WAMPUM: beads, pierced and strung, used by Indians as money or for ornaments

Land Ho!

European explorers began making their way into the West Virginia area in the late 1600s. Most of them were English, but people from Germany, Switzerland, and France also explored the beautiful mountain country. They found many rivers and streams, including the New River, which flows west instead of east toward the Atlantic Ocean. Large numbers of animals, especially elk, were found, too.

Thomas Batts and Robert Fallam led an exploration into western Virginia in 1671. They found trees with the letters MANI carved in the trunks. They never discovered what this meant, or who put it there!

Home, Sweet Home

Most of West Virginia's early settlers did not come from Virginia, but rather the other colonies, including New York, Pennsylvania, Delaware, New Jersey, and Maryland.

In 1727, a group of German-speaking people from Pennsylvania settled in an area they called Mecklenburg. The town's name was changed in 1798 to Shepherdstown to honor its founder, Thomas Shepherd. This became official in 1867. The influence of these people we call the Pennsylvania Dutch is still evident in present-day Shepherdstown. You can see samples of their artworks on the sides of barns.

There's Coal in Them Thar Hills!

When John Peter Salling discovered coal near the present-day village of Peytona in 1742, he literally changed the complexion of West Virginia. Coal would become king in West Virginia. By 1870, the state's mines were putting out 600,000 tons (544,311 metric tons) of the black mineral.

Coal Mining

The prospect of making a profitable living attracted families from southern and eastern Europe. However, they soon learned that most of the wealth went to a privileged few known as "coal barons."

Coal miners worked in some of the worst conditions imaginable—18-hour days in less-than-sturdy, pitch-dark shafts. They paid huge rents for shacks and high prices for supplies at the company store. At the end of the day, exhausted miners would spill forth from the shafts covered with black dust inside and out. Many miners died from a disease called black lung directly related to breathing the black dust all day.

John Henry—
The Hard-Hammering Hero

West Virginia's coal mines have also produced its greatest legend—John Henry. The story goes that John Henry weighed 44 pounds (20 kilograms), was black as night, and had a preacher's booming voice when he was born!

He became so strong he could drive a hole in a mountain big enough for a train to go through and could lay 90 miles (145 kilometers) of track in one day without even taking a deep breath.

One day, the boss brought in a steam drill that could do the work of 10 men, so John Henry challenged it. He started on one side of the mountain, and the steam drill on the other. When they met, John Henry had drilled more than a mile and the drill only a quarter of a mile. People cheered as John Henry came out of the tunnel. Then he closed his eyes and fell down dead. He had hammered so hard and so long that his big heart had burst!

Freedom! Freedom!

Some settlers in the New World felt that England ignored their ideas and concerns. In 1775, the colonies went to war with England. On July 4, 1776, the Declaration of Independence was signed.

Revolution

Western Virginia did not become involved in the Revolutionary War until 1777—a time the settlers referred to as "the bloody year of the three sevens." Even then the settlers were not fighting the British themselves but Indians whom the British had lured to their side. On the east coast, American militiamen were battling the redcoats as those in western Virginia were taking on Indians armed with British weapons and trained by British officers.

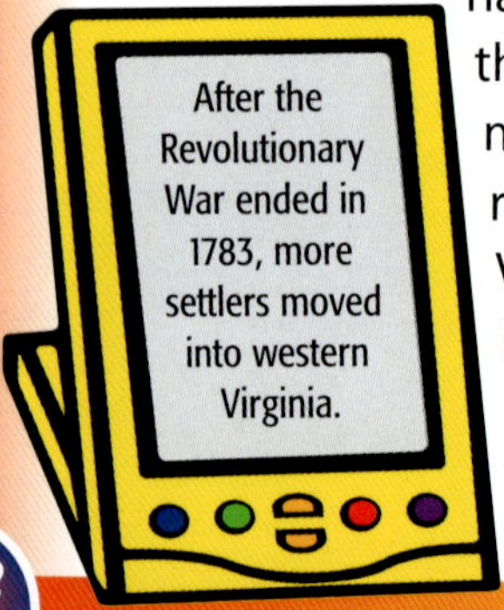

After the Revolutionary War ended in 1783, more settlers moved into western Virginia.

Slaves and Slavery

While the large plantations of eastern Virginia were worked by many African-American slaves, the mountainous region of western Virginia did not lend itself to large farms. There was no need for slaves. In fact, while a third of eastern Virginia's population were slaves, only 4 percent of the western part of the state was inhabited by slaves. Many people in western Virginia didn't think slavery was beneficial to the economy at all since slaves were taking jobs that white workers could be paid to perform.

In 1865, the 13th Amendment abolished slavery in the United States.

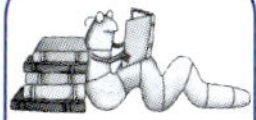

Word Definition

ABOLITIONIST: person who believed slavery was wrong and should be ended

The Civil War

Brother

The Civil War was fought between the American states. The argument was over states' rights to make their own decisions, including whether or not to own slaves. Some of the southern states began to secede (leave) the Union. They formed the Confederate States of America.

When Virginia decided to leave the Union, the western counties held mass protest meetings and decided to break off to create their own state. At first the area was called the Restored Government of Virginia, and two years later, it became the 35th state.

During the Civil War, a number of battles were fought in West Virginia. The town of Romney changed hands 56 times!

Word Definition

RECONSTRUCTION: the recovery and rebuilding period following the Civil War

vs. Brother

The Civil War was also called the War Between the States. Soldiers often found themselves fighting against former friends and neighbors, even brother against brother. Those who did survive often went home without an arm, leg, or both, since amputation was the "cure" for most battlefield wounds. More Americans were killed during the Civil War than during World Wars I and II together!

In 1863, the Emancipation Proclamation, given by U.S. President Abraham Lincoln, freed the slaves still under Confederate control. Some slaves became sharecroppers; others went to Northern states to work in factories.

Get It In Writing!

1763
King George III of Britain's
Proclamation of 1763

1768
Treaty of Fort Stanwix

1775
Treaty of Pittsburgh

1776
Declaration of Independence

1789
U.S. Constitution

1794
Treaty of Greenville

1872
West Virginia state constitution

Welcome To America!

People have come to West Virginia from other states and many other countries on almost every continent! As time goes by, West Virginia's population grows more diverse. This means that people of different races and from different cultures and ethnic backgrounds have moved to West Virginia.

In the past, many immigrants have come to West Virginia from Europe. More recently, people have migrated to West Virginia from Hispanic countries such as Mexico. Only a certain number of immigrants are allowed to move to America each year. Many of these immigrants eventually become U.S. citizens.

1907

Explosion at Monongah Mine kills 361 miners in worst mining disaster in U.S. history

1914

Eccles mine explosion kills 188

1920

Labor dispute over poor working conditions between miners and guards leaves 15 dead, dozens injured in Matewan

1924

Mine accident in Benwood kills 119

1944

Tornadoes strike five West Virginia counties, killing 100, injuring 381

1968

Coal mine in Farmington explodes, killing 78 miners

1972

Dams along Buffalo Creek collapse; 125 die

Legal Stuff

1776

Settlers in West Virginia petition Virginia for their own government

1871

Law restores voting rights to Confederate veterans; Virginia loses lawsuit to regain Jefferson and Berkeley counties

1890

West Virginia workers begin joining United Mine Workers of America union

1915

U.S. Supreme Court makes West Virginia pay Virginia more than $12 million as part of debt owed to Virginia from when West Virginia became a separate state

1956

West Virginia becomes the last state in the nation to allow women to serve on juries in trials

1985

West Virginia sets up state lottery

1868

The Married Women's Property Act allows married women to own property in certain circumstances

1928

First African-American woman to serve in U.S. legislature, Minnie Buckingham Harper, is appointed to West Virginia's house of delegates

1907

Anna Jarvis creates Mother's Day, holding the first celebration on May 12

1931

West Virginia inventor and yo-yo tycoon Don Duncan makes a deal with newspaper tycoon William Randolph Hearst to advertise yo-yo contests. To be eligible to compete, contestants, usually children, have to sell newspaper subscriptions. In two months, more than 50,000 newspaper subscriptions are sold

Fight! Fight! Fight!

West Virginians took part in these wars:

- French and Indian Wars
- Revolutionary War
- War of 1812
- Mexican-American War
- Civil War
- Spanish-American War
- World War I
- World War II
- Korean War
- Vietnam War
- Persian Gulf War

A FINE STATE FOR THE SHAPE IT'S IN

When you look at the outline of the state of West Virginia, it may conjure up the image of a frog jumping toward the south with its back legs extended. These two "frog legs" are known as West Virginia's panhandles. West Virginia is the only state with two panhandles.

The main contributors to West Virginia's irregular outline are the Appalachian Mountains on the east and the Ohio River to the west.

Speaking of those mountains, West Virginia is the only state that lies in its entirety within the Appalachian chain.

An old West Virginia joke is that West Virginia is a fine state—considering the shape it's in!

Indian Tribes

- Adena
- Hopewell
- Iroquois
- Tuscarora
- Mingo
- Shawnee
- Delaware
- Cherokee

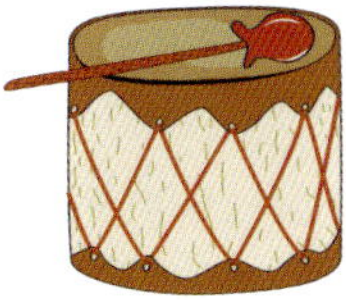

When settlers began arriving in the western part of the state, the number of Indians decreased dramatically as a result of diseases like smallpox and invasions from more violent tribes like the Iroquois, Cherokee, and Shawnee.

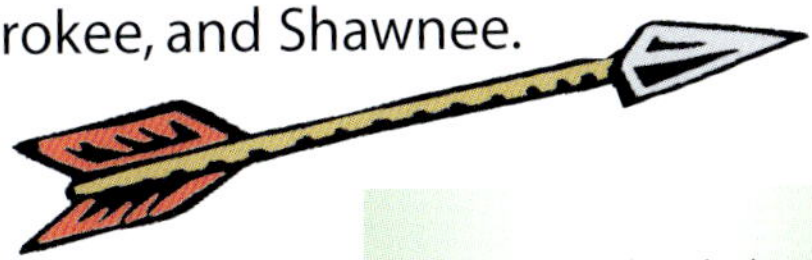

West Virginia's earliest inhabitants were mound builders.

The Indians of West Virginia could not have known that the coming of the white man would mean an end to the way of life they had known for hundreds of years.

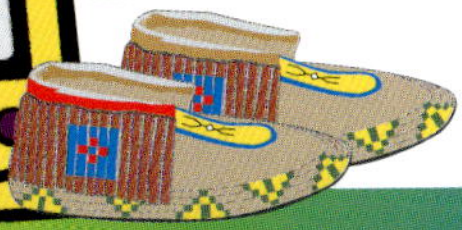

Here, There, Everywhere!

JOHN LEDERER—a German geographer; the first European to explore what is now West Virginia after he was hired in 1669 by Sir William Berkeley, governor of the Virginia Colony

THOMAS BATTS and ROBERT FALLAM—explorers, who in 1671, led an expedition through the Appalachian Mountains, reaching the New River

JOHN P. SALLING and JOHN HOWARD—were the first to note the discovery of coal they found in the Coal River in 1742

GEORGE WASHINGTON—was among a party of surveyors in West Virginia when he was 16 in 1748, crossing the Allegheny Mountains

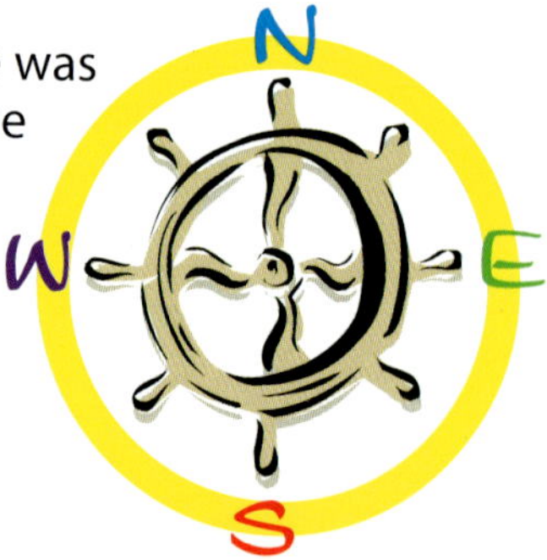

Founding Fathers

DANIEL BOONE—came to the Kanawha Valley in 1788 when the area was still a wild frontier; settled in 1791 near what would become Charleston

FRANCIS H. PIERPONT—named governor of the Restored Government of Virginia in 1861 and helped form the independent state of West Virginia; called the "father of West Virginia"

MORGAN AP MORGAN—pioneer from Delaware who became the first white settler in West Virginia by building a log cabin near Bunker Hill

Founding Mothers

MARY INGLES—pioneer woman captured by the Shawnee in 1755 who managed to escape and make her way back to her home; she noted land formations between the Blue Ridge Mountains and Ohio River, which helped future settlers

BETTY ZANE—young woman who dashed through gunfire to retrieve a supply of gunpowder during a battle with Indians in 1777

ANN BAILEY—scout, Indian fighter, and sharpshooter who was nicknamed "Mad Ann" Bailey after she rode 100 miles (161 kilometers) through dense underbrush to deliver gunpowder to a fort during an Indian siege

DADDY SMITH—a slave; in a major battle in 1777 singlehandedly defended a key wall at Fort Henry

MARTIN ROBINSON DELANY—abolitionist, soldier, and physician; born in Charleston; with Frederick Douglass, he founded *The North Star* newspaper; in 1865, became the first black major in the U.S. Army

BOOKER T. WASHINGTON—grew up in Malden; became an educator and founded Tuskegee Institute; social reformer who believed blacks should seek employment and education rather than expect social equality with whites

NNAMDI AZIKIWE—alumnus from Harpers Ferry Storer College; became the first president of the Republic of Nigeria

ELIZABETH SIMPSON DREWRY—first African-American woman to serve in the West Virginia legislature

CARTER GODWIN WOODSON—historian born to former slaves in what is today West Virginia; known as "the father of black history"

DID SOMEONE SAY BOO!?

Harpers Ferry Hauntings

They say that some days you can see a tall, slim, white-haired man with a small, black dog pacing the streets of Harpers Ferry, West Virginia. Many notice his resemblance to the fiery abolitionist John Brown, who was hanged after he went on a murderous raid, intent on ending slavery and freeing all slaves. Some ask if they can have their photograph taken with him, but when the film is developed, they see no man beside them. The man continues on his journey to the door of the fire-engine house, where he mysteriously vanishes.

They also say that the ghost of one of the men in John Brown's band can be seen in Harpers Ferry as well. After he was captured by an angry mob, he was mutilated and his body thrown in a pen with hogs. His tortured soul still roams the area.

Then there's the story of the haunted church, which was hit by a mortar during a Civil War battle. A priest strangely disappears into walls, and some have claimed to hear a baby crying on the front steps...even when there's no baby there!

DO YOU BELIEVE IN GHOSTS?

RANDY BARNES—world-record shotputter from Charleston; won a gold medal in the 1996 Olympics

GEORGE BRETT—Glen Dale native; played professional baseball, including winning the 1980 Most Valuable Player award

SELVA LEWIS "LEW" BURDETTE—professional baseball pitcher; born in Nitro; won more than 200 games in his career

ROBERT LEE "STAN" HUFF—professional football Hall of Famer from Edna Gas

GINO MARCHETTI—Smithers native, professional football Hall of Famer

CHRISTY MARTIN—professional female boxer

MARY LOU RETTON—gymnast from Fairmont; won a gold medal in the 1984 Olympics

NATALIE TENNANT—Fairview native; became the first female to serve as West Virginia University's Mountaineer mascot amid protests from some students and alumni

GEORGEANN WELLS—first woman to dunk a basketball during a college game when she was playing for West Virginia University

JERRY WEST—Cheylan native; first professional basketball player to score more than 4,000 playoff points

STEVE YEAGER—professional baseball player from Huntington

Entertainers

BELLE BOYD—author, actress, and Confederate spy; born in Martinsburg

BERNIE CASEY—professional football player and actor; born in Wyco

PHYLLIS CURTIN—operatic soprano from Clarksburg; performed with the Metropolitan Opera

DAGMAR—comedienne; born in Huntington

JOANNE DRU—actress from Logan

DON KNOTTS—actor from Morgantown

PETER MARSHALL—game show host from Huntington

KATHY MATTEA—country music singer from South Charleston

ELEANOR STEBER—operatic soprano from Wheeling

CHARLES McCOY—Oak Hill native; musician and music director for *Hee Haw*

DON REDMAN—band leader, composer, born in Piedmont

SOUPY SALES—radio and television comedian; grew up in Huntington

JEFF STEVENS—country music songwriter from Alum Creek

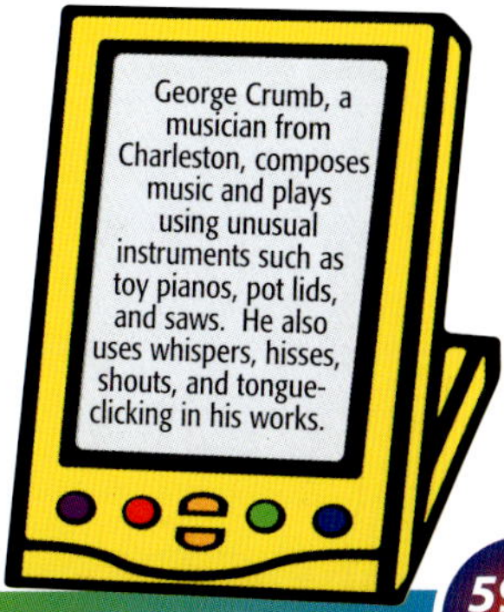

Authors

- **PEARL S. BUCK**—Nobel and Pulitzer prize-winning author from Hillsboro
- **BETSY BYARS**—Newbery Award-winning author who lives in Morgantown
- **STEPHEN COONTS**—best-selling author from Morgantown
- **REBECCA HARDING DAVIS**—Civil War era writer; lived in Wheeling and wrote of the hardships of working people and small farmers in West Virginia
- **JOHN KNOWLES**—Fairmont author
- **MARGARET PRESCOTT MONTAGUE**—White Sulphur Springs native; wrote short stories depicting mountain life

- **MELVILLE DAVISSON POST**—renowned mystery writer from Romines Mill
- **MARY LEE SETTLE**—Charleston author; wrote a four-volume history of West Virginia and novels
- **HUBERT SKIDMORE**—author born on Laurel Mountain; works include realistic pictures of mountain people

Artists

PAULA CLENDENIN—painter and printmaker from Charleston; works blend the mountains and figures in energetic portrayals

ELLIOT DAINGERFIELD—artist from Harpers Ferry; became well known for his landscapes and figure studies

C.E. HAWORTH—composer from Huntington; works are often played during Episcopal church services

ALISON HELM—sculptor from Morgantown; works with steel and wood

CARA JAYE—Morgantown photographer; focuses on the female figure in her work

ELEAZER HUTCHINSON MILLER—Shepherdstown artist known for illustrating such books as *Tom O'Shanter* and *Song of the Sea*

ROGER PRICE—Charleston actor, artist; created *Droodles*, simple drawings with humorous captions

CHERYL TOTH—painter from Winfield; works are abstract expressions relying on her use of line, color, and movement

HAROLD TUCKER WEBSTER—Parkersburg native; cartoon character Caspar Milquetoast was featured in *The Timid Soul* comic strip

What would you get if you mixed Roger Price's cartoons with those of Harold Tucker Webster?

Droodles of Milquetoast

Very Important People

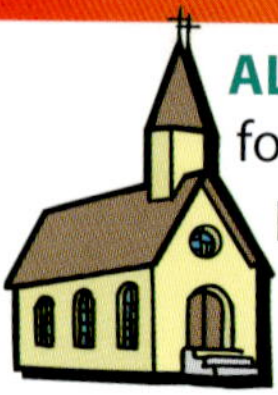

ALEXANDER CAMPBELL—minister who founded the Disciples of Christ church; published the *Christian Baptist*, West Virginia's first religious publication

JOSEPH H. DISS DEBAR—artist who lived in Doddridge County and designed West Virginia's state seal and coat of arms; put together the first *Handbook of West Virginia*

THOMAS "STONEWALL" JACKSON—Confederate general who was known for his brilliant strategies during the Civil War; born in Clarksburg

KARL SPENCER LASHLEY—Davis-born psychologist; studied the human brain's functions in relation to human behavior

GEORGE ARMITAGE MILLER—psychologist; pioneered work in psycholinguistics

Very Important People

WALTER REUTHER—Wheeling native; president of the United Auto Workers union for nearly 25 years; engineered the merger of the American Federation of Labor (AFL) and the Congress of Industrial Organizations (CIO)

JAMES RUMSEY—inventor of the steamboat; first demonstrated it on the Potomac River at Shepherdstown in 1787

ISRAEL CHARLES WHITE—geologist from Monongalia County; conducted surveys to determine the geological and economic impact of the state's natural resources

More Very Important People

CHIEF LOGAN—Mingo chief; worked to keep peace between the Indians and the settlers…until his own family was murdered, and then he began attacking settlers

CHIEF CORNSTALK—Shawnee chief; took up arms to aid Chief Logan in Lord Dunmore's War

MAJOR SAMUEL McCULLOCH—a leader in one of the battles of 1777; escaped from a band of Indians by urging his horse to leap off a tall cliff; he and the horse both survived

HENRY GASSAWAY DAVIS—industrialist; at age 80, financed the building of the Potomac and Piedmont Railroad

MARY HARRIS "MOTHER" JONES—Irish-born woman; aided striking coal miners by organizing the United Mine Workers of America and encouraging strikers to avoid being violent

Political Leaders

ARTHUR INGRAM BOREMAN—first governor of West Virginia; opposed Virginia seceding from the Union; supported West Virginia separating from Virginia

ROBERT C. BYRD—re-elected to the Senate five times with the greatest margin of victory in West Virginia history; famous for his fiddle-playing

JOHN WILLIAM DAVIS—U.S. representative from Clarksburg; as a lawyer, argued more cases before the U.S. Supreme Court than any other attorney

THOMAS EWING—from West Liberty; first U.S. secretary of the interior

MINNIE BUCKINGHAM HARPER—from Welch; first black woman legislator in the United States, who filled her husband's slot in the House of Delegates following his death

JOHN EDWARD KENNA—represents West Virginia in U.S. Capitol's Statuary Hall; led push to make Charleston the state capital

MATTHEW M. NEELY—Fairmont-born governor; pushed for labor and mining reforms for state residents

CYRUS VANCE—Clarksburg native; served as diplomat under President Lyndon B. Johnson and as secretary of state to President Jimmy Carter

GOOD GUY

SID HATFIELD—police chief of Matewan who defended the rights of poor, exploited coal miners in the early 20th century

BAD GUYS

HARRY FORD SINCLAIR—Wheeling native who founded Sinclair Oil but was best known for his involvement in the Teapot Dome oil field scandal

JOHN BROWN—abolitionist; believed God had handpicked him to end slavery by starting a revolt and releasing all slaves to join him; after murderous rebellion, was captured in Harpers Ferry, tried, and hanged; called martyr by some, murderer by others

CHARLES MANSON—leader of a hippie commune in California; convinced his followers to murder innocent victims; spent much of his youth as a juvenile delinquent in West Virginia

HERO

CHUCK YEAGER—Myra native who was the first person to travel faster than the speed of sound; during his military career in World War II, he shot down 13 enemy German aircraft

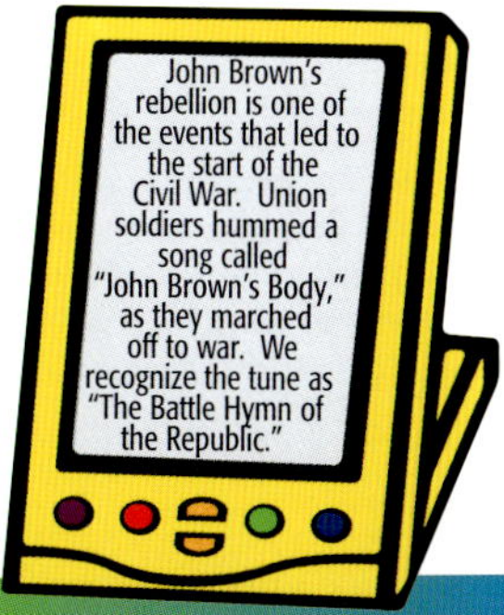

Keeping the Faith

CHURCHES

St. Peter's Catholic Church, Harpers Ferry
Morgan's Chapel, Bunker Hill
Christ Church, Bunker Hill
Old Fields Church, north of Moorefield
East Run Church, Fairmont
Tygarts Valley Presbyterian Church, Huttonsville
Rehoboth Church, Union
Virginia's Chapel, Cedar Grove
African Zion Church, Malden
Kanawha Saline Presbyterian Church, Malden
Bethany Church of Christ, Bethany
Old Stone Presbyterian Church, Lewisburg
Andrews Methodist Church, Grafton
St. Michael's Church, Bulltown
Wesley Chapel, Buckhannon
Palace of Gold, Adena
Our Lady of the Pines, Cathedral State Park
Father's Day Church, **Central United Methodist Church**, Fairmont

SCHOOLS

Storer College, Harpers Ferry
Bethany College, Bethany
West Virginia Wesleyan Chapel, Buckhannon
West Virginia University, Morgantown
Concord College, Athens
Marshall University, Huntington
Shepherd College, Shepherdstown
West Virginia State College, Institute
University of Charleston, Charleston
Wheeling Jesuit College, Wheeling
Davis and Elkins College, Elkins
Alderson-Broaddus College, Philippi
West Virginia Canine College, Buckhannon

NATIONAL SITES

Harpers Ferry National Historic Park, Harpers Ferry
Chesapeake and Ohio Canal National Historical Park, Potomac River
Appalachian National Scenic Trail
Bluestone National Scenic River, southern West Virginia
Gauley River National Recreation Area
New River Gorge National River
Monongahela National Forest
George Washington National Forest
Jefferson National Forest

STATE PARKS

Berkeley Springs State Park, Berkeley
Lost River State Park, Fort Ashby
Cathedral State Park, Thomas
Pricketts Fort State Park, north of Fairmont
Mason Dixon Historical Park, northwest of Morgantown
Coopers Rock State Forest, east of Morgantown
Watters Smith State Park, west of Clarkburg
Cass Scenic Railroad State Park, Cass
Babcock State Park, Fayetteville
Hawk's Nest State Park, Ansted
Blennerhassett Island Historical Park, Blennerhassett Island
Grave Creek Mound State Park, Moundsville

Home, Sweet Home!

Historical Homes

Morgan Cabin, Bunker Hill

Campbell Mansion, Bethany

Harewood, Charles Town

Harper House, Harpers Ferry

Berkeley Castle, Berkeley

Light-Horse Harry Lee Cabin, Fort Ashby

Job Prickett House, Pricketts Fort State Park

High Gate, Fairmont

The Old Stone House, Morgantown

Stealey-Goff-Vance House, Clarksburg

Henry McWhorter Cabin, Jacksons Mill

Halliehurst, Elkins

Home, Sweet Home!

John A. North House, Lewisburg

Jessie B. Bowlin House, Lewisburg

Contentment, Ansted

Craik-Patton House, Charleston

Torquilstone, Charleston

Alexander Campbell Mansion, Wheeling

General Adam Stephen House, Martinsburg

Belle Boyd House, Martinsburg

Cunningham Farmhouse, Bulltown

A few of West Virginia's famous Battlefields

- **Droop Mountain Battlefield State Park, Droop Mountain**—site of the last major Civil War battle in West Virginia on November 6, 1863
- **Bulltown**—site of 12-hour Civil War skirmish on October 13, 1863
- **Carnifex Ferry Battlefield State Park**, Carnifex Ferry—site of Civil War battle on September 10, 1861
- **Point Pleasant Battle Monument State Park**—site where battle of more than 2,000 Indians and settlers occurred on October 10, 1774
- **The covered bridge, near Philippi**—site of the first Civil War battle in West Virginia

A few of West Virginia's famous Forts

- **Fort Ashby, Fort Ashby**—large log structure built in 1755 by order of George Washington
- **The Barracks, Lewisburg**—log structure built by British troops before the American Revolution; housed American soldiers during the War of 1812
- **Fort New Salem, Salem**—reconstructed Appalachian pioneer settlement

Libraries

Check out the following special West Virginia libraries! (Do you have a library card? Have you worn it out yet?!)

Public Library, Shepherdstown

Gray Barker UFO Collection, Clarksburg. The Harrison County Library in Clarksburg houses a large collection of materials devoted to UFO research. The collector, Gray Barker, has also written a number of books about UFOs, including *They Knew Too Much about Flying Saucers, Gray Barker at Giant Rock, The Sliver Bridge,* and *MIB—The Secret Terror Among Us.*

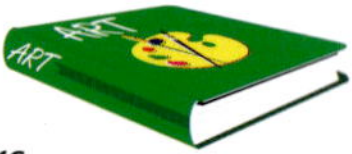

Greenbrier County Library, Lewisburg

Craft Memorial Library, Bluefield

West Virginia State Library, Charleston

Parkersburg Carnegie Public Library

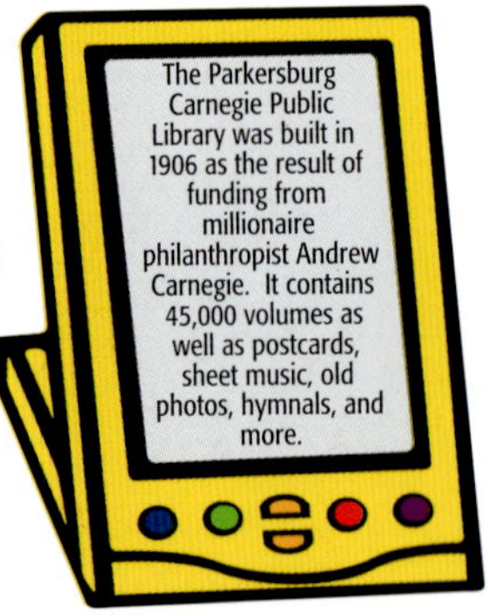

Zoos and Attractions

Cranberry Wilderness, Cranberry Mountain—protected natural area that includes cranberry bogs and rare plant species

National Radio Astronomy Observatory, north of Cass

Oglebay Park, Wheeling—site with gardens, greenhouses, glass museum, the Good Children's Zoo

National Fisheries Center, Leetown

Greenland Gap Nature Preserve, Mineral County

Edray Trout Hatchery, Marlinton—site where visitors can see all the Mountain State's species of trout

West Virginia State Wildlife Center, south of Buckhannon

Ohio River Islands National Wildlife Refuge, St. Marys

Core Arboretum, West Virginia University, Morgantown

Museums

Snodgrass One-Room Schoolhouse Museum, Fairmont
Randolph County Historical Society Museum, Beverly
Cass History Museum, Cass
Pearl S. Buck Birthplace Museum, Hillsboro
President's Cottage, Greenbrier Hotel, White Sulphur Springs
Monroe County Historical Society Museum, Union
West Virginia State Museum, Charleston
Sunrise Museum, Charleston
Blennerhassett Museum, Blennerhassett Island
Harpers Ferry Toy Train Museum, Harpers Ferry
Coal Museum, Beckley
Museum of Berkeley Springs, Berkeley Springs
Triple Brick Museum, Martinsburg
James Rumsey Steamboat Museum, Shepherdstown
Delf Norona Museum, Moundsville
Americana Museum, Aurora

Lest We Forget

MONUMENTS

James Rumsey Memorial Monument, Shepherdstown

Morgan Monument, Bunker Hill

Statue of John Henry, Talcott

MEMORIALS

West Virginia Miner's Memorial, Monongah

Nancy Hanks Memorial, Saddle Mountain—site where Abraham Lincoln's mother was born

International Mother's Day Shrine, Grafton

Statue of "Devil" Anse Hatfield, Hatfield Family Cemetery, Sarah Anne

MARKER

John Brown Gallows, Harpers Ferry

The Arts

Old Opera House Theatre Company, Charles Town

Boarman Art Center, Martinsburg

Apollo Civic Theater, Martinsburg

Stifel Fine Art Center, Wheeling

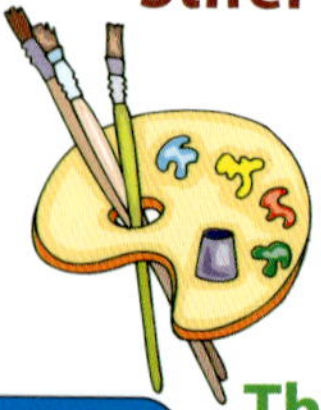

Huntington Museum of Art, Huntington

Theatre West Virginia, Beckley

The Appalachian Gallery, Morgantown

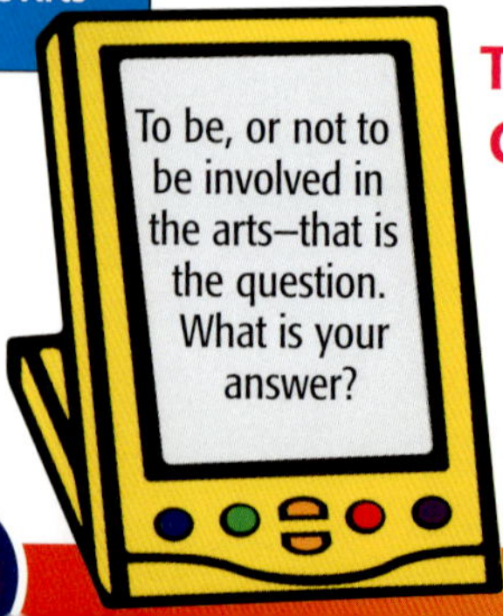

Just Milling Around!

Bunker Hill Flour Mill, Bunker Hill

Shepherd's Grist Mill, Shepherdstown

Lyon's Mill, Fort Ashby

Blaker's Mill, Jacksons Mill

Glade Creek Grist Mill, Babcock State Park

Roads,

James River-Kanawha Turnpike (Route 60)

Greenbrier River Trail, Elk River

West Virginia Turnpike, from Charleston to Princeton

Bridges,

Van Metre Ford Bridge, Martinsburg

Barrackville Covered Bridge, Fairmont

New River Gorge Bridge, Fayetteville

Wheeling Suspension Bridge, Wheeling

Indian Creek Covered Bridge, Hinton

Covered Bridge, Philippi

Locust Creek Covered Bridge, Hillsboro

Fish Creek Covered Bridge, Hundred

East End Bridge, Huntington

and More!

Henry Clay Iron Furnace, east of Morgantown

Criel Mound, South Charleston

Grave Creek Mound, Moundsville

The Pringle Tree, Buckhannon

Caves and Caverns

Lost World Caverns, Lewisburg—contains large rooms with magnificent stalagmite and stalactite formations

Smoke Hole Caverns, Petersburg—contains one of the world's longest ribbon stalactites, a lake, and a stream

Organ Cave, near Lewisburg—used by Confederate General Robert E. Lee as an ammunition storage site; has a stalactite formation that looks like a pipe organ that makes musical sounds when struck

Question:

- Which is the stalagmite?
- Which is the stalactite?

ANSWER: Stalactites are long, tapering formations hanging from the roof of a cavern, produced by continuous watery deposits containing certain minerals. The mineral-rich water dripping from stalactites often forms conical stalagmites on the floor below.

Word Definition

SPELUNKER: a person who goes exploring caves for fun

West Virginia's Animals Include:

Red-bellied snake
Copperhead
Timber rattlesnake
Bobcat
Black bear
Eastern chipmunk
White-tailed deer
Raccoon
Virginia opossum
Eastern cottontail

Short-tailed shrew
American toad
Common garter snake
Gray squirrel
Southern flying squirrel
Little brown bat
Red salamander

Red-bellied snakes are shy reptiles that curl their upper lips when frightened. Females don't lay eggs, but give birth to live babies. The underside of a red-bellied snake can be orange, yellow, or even black, in addition to red!

Some endangered West Virginia animals are:

Take a Walk on the Wild Side!

Indiana bat
Virginia big-eared bat
Clubshell
American peregrine falcon
Fanshell
Ring pink mussel
Pink mucket pearlymussel
Tubercled-blossom pearlymussel
Northern riffleshell
James River spinymussel
Virginia northern flying squirrel

Strip mining and pollution from the chemical industry have taken their toll on West Virginia's wildlife. Most large animal species have disappeared, but new conservation methods are in place to hopefully bring back some animals.

Birds

You may spy these birds in West Virginia:

- Mourning dove
- American robin
- House wren
- Screech-owl
- Northern cardinal
- Downy woodpecker
- Wild turkey
- Brown thrasher
- Eagle
- Falcon
- Hawk
- Quail
- Scarlet tanager
- Snipe
- Hummingbird
- Wood thrush
- Wood duck
- Black-winged blackbird
- Green-backed heron

A hummingbird's wings beat 75 times a second—so fast that you only see a blur! They make short squeaky sounds, but do not sing.

Don't let these West Virginia bugs bug you!

Dragonfly
Giant water bug
Diving beetle
Whirligig beetle
Mosquito
Ladybug beetle
Mayfly
Damselfly
Band-winged grasshopper
Katydid
Field cricket
Praying mantis
Stick insect
Periodical cicada
Spittlebug
Ant lion
Tiger swallowtail

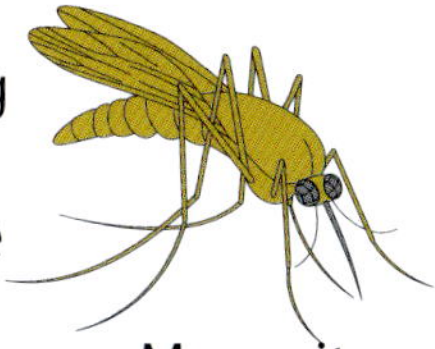
Mosquito

Ladybug

Praying Mantis

Tiger Swallowtail

Field cricket

Fish

Swimming in West Virginia's waters:

- Minnow
- Bullhead
- Catfish
- Bluegill sunfish
- Bass
- Crappie
- Muskellunge
- Pickerel
- Trout
- Walleyed pike

In West Virginia's ponds, you may find:

Hydra
Leech
Freshwater mussel
Pond snail
Freshwater eel
Common musk turtle
Painted turtle
Mud puppy
Water snake
American toad
Eastern newt
Cricket frog
Bullfrog

Rocks and Minerals

Minerals are the building blocks of all rocks. Most minerals are tiny and you need a magnifying glass to see them clearly. Some minerals you may find in West Virginia include:

Augite	Kaolinite
Iron Pyrite	Mica
Quartz	Hornblende
Calcite	Olivin
Feldspar	

Rocks are solid masses of minerals or rock fragments that occur in nature. Some rocks you may find in West Virginia include:

Granite	Chert	Quartzite
Pegmatite	Schist	Meteorites
Conglomerate	Slate	
Coal	Gneiss	
Limestone	Marble	
Flint	Slate	

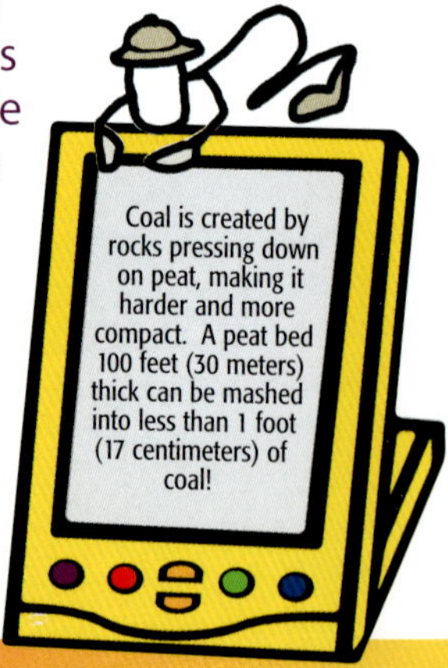

TREEMENDOUS!

THESE TREES TOWER OVER WEST VIRGINIA:

Beech
Cherry
Hemlock
Hickory
Maple
Oak
Poplar
Red spruce
White pine

Wildflowers

Are you crazy about these West Virginia flowers?

Aster
Azalea
Black-eyed Susan
Bloodroot
Butter-and-eggs
Dogwood
Hepatica
Redbud
Rhododendron
Wild crab apple
Goldenrod
White-blossomed hawthorn

Cream of the Crops

Agricultural products from West Virginia:

BEEF CATTLE

DAIRY PRODUCTS

APPLES

CORN

CHICKENS

TOBACCO

HAY

TURKEYS

PEACHES

The first free rural mail delivery started in Charles Town, West Virginia on October 6, 1896.

The first Union soldier killed in the Civil War was Bailey Brown, who died at Fetterman, West Virginia, on May 22, 1861.

West Virginia has the **highest average elevation** of any state east of the Mississippi River.

The Mingo Oak, the **oldest and largest white oak** tree in the United States, was declared dead and cut down in a special ceremony on September 30, 1938. Its age was estimated at 582 years.

The **first building dedicated to World War I veterans** was dedicated in Welch, West Virginia, on May 30, 1923.

Charleston's Virginia Street's 1500 block has been called the **longest city block** in the world.

The **only residence built entirely of coal** is Coal House in White Sulphur Springs, West Virginia.

Memorial Tunnel in West Virginia was the **first tunnel to be monitored by television**.

In 1883, **the first steel cut nails** were made in West Virginia.

Festivals

Celebrate!!!

MAPLE SYRUP FESTIVAL, in Pickens in March

ALPINE FESTIVAL, held in Davis each March

FEAST OF THE RAMSOM, in Richwood each April

STRAWBERRY FESTIVAL, held in Buckhannon in May

WEBSTER WOODCHOPPING FESTIVAL, held in May

WEST VIRGINIA STATE FOLK FESTIVAL in Glenville in June

BLUEGRASS COUNTRY MUSIC FESTIVAL in Summersville each summer

APPALACHIAN ARTS AND CRAFTS FESTIVAL in Beckley in late August

AUGUSTA HERITAGE FESTIVAL in Elkins in August

CHERRY RIVER FESTIVAL in Richwood in August

POTATO FESTIVAL in Summersville, Labor Day weekend

ITALIAN HERITAGE FESTIVAL in Clarksburg in September

PRESTON COUNTY BUCKWHEAT FESTIVAL in Kingwood in September

WEST VIRGINIA OIL AND GAS FESTIVAL in Sistersville in September

BLACK WALNUT FESTIVAL in Spencer in October

WEST VIRGINIA MOLASSES FESTIVAL in Arnoldsburg in October

MOUNTAIN STATE FOREST FESTIVAL in Elkins in October

WINTER FESTIVAL OF LIGHTS in Wheeling from early November until early January

Holidays

Calendar

Martin Luther King, Jr. Day, *3rd Monday in January*	Groundhog Day, *February 2*	Presidents' Day, *3rd Monday in February*
Memorial Day, *last Monday in May*	Independence Day, *July 4*	Labor Day, *1st Monday in September*
Columbus Day, *2nd Monday in October*	Veterans Day, *November 11*	Thanksgiving, *4th Thursday in November*

Christmas, Hanukkah, Kwanzaa, Vietnamese Tet, and Chinese New Year are all special celebrations in West Virginia.

Famous Food

West Virginia is famous for...

...the following foods!

Applesauce	Cheese	Sauerbraten
Apple butter	Maple syrup	Stout country soup
Bratwurst	Molasses	Trout
Calzones	Pancakes	Chili topped
Fried chicken	Pepperoni roll	with coleslaw
Fried ramps	Pickled beets	*Pfeffernusse*, a
Carbonara	Potatoes	ginger cookie

West Virginia Works!

West Virginia has a diverse economy with several major industries including mining, manufacturing, and agriculture.

Salt mining was once West Virginia's leading industry, but that changed to coal mining. Today, coal is still the state's most valuable resource, but West Virginia is third behind Kentucky and Wyoming in coal production.

Glassmaking has also been important to West Virginia's economy. The Blenko Glass Company in Milton is especially well known for its production of stained glass. The Washington National Cathedral in Washington, D.C., and the Cathedral of St. John the Divine in New York City feature breathtaking examples of Blenko glass.

Tourism has become the most important industry in West Virginia. The state's excellent rivers and rapids attract 200,000 rafters each year!

Because of its mountainous terrain, agriculture accounts for only 1 percent of the state's economy. Livestock is the top agricultural product, with broiler chickens being the most profitable.

Books & Websites

My First Book About West Virginia by Carole Marsh
America the Beautiful: West Virginia by Wende Fazio
Kids Learn America by Patricia Gordon and Reed C. Snow
From Sea to Shining Sea: West Virginia by Dennis Fradin
Let's Discover the States: West Virginia by the Aylesworths
The West Virginia Experience Series by Carole Marsh

West Virginia Glossary

Glossary Words

abolitionist—a person who opposes slavery

barge—a large flat-bottomed boat used for carrying goods on rivers or canals

feud—a bitter quarrel that lasts a long time and usually occurs between two families

gristmill—a mill where grains are ground

hillbilly—a person who lives in or comes from the mountains or backwoods of the South

panhandle—a strip of land that looks, on a map, like the handle of a pan

ramps—wild leeks, which are relatives to onions

ravines—long, deep hollows worn by streams of water

secede—to stop being a member of a group